A Gift For:

Becky

From:

Annie

mommy
prayers

TRACY MAYOR

HYPERION

For Tom, Connor, and Will—
the answer to all my prayers

CONTENTS

Prayers
for Sleepless Nights

Prayers for Meltdown Moments and Other Stressful Situations

Prayers for
Special Days and
Special People

prayers for

Crazy Days

PRAYER

for the Binky

Dear God, Please help me find my baby's binky. I know they're bad for dental development. I know they encourage early weaning and ear infections. None of that matters right now. Please, Lord, send me a vision: Show me where the damn binky is! It's 5:15 in the morning and I must stop this kid from crying before the whole house is up. Is it in the dusty corner under the crib? Wedged into the side cushions of the stroller? Underneath the car seat? In the right footie of my baby's snowsuit, which is where I found my keys last week? Please, God, give me a hint, bestow on me the clarity of mind to remember where I last saw the binky. And quick. Amen.

PRAYER

for My Five-Minute Shower

○

Dear God, I am not asking for much here, just five kid-free minutes to myself. I'm not asking for a *good* shower—the one where you shave your legs and pumice your heels and slather your limbs with sea-salt-lemon-mimosa foaming body scrub and exfoliate whatever bits need exfoliating. Nothing like that. Just five minutes under a stream of hot water so I can shampoo the ick out of my hair, slop on a little conditioner, swipe my face with one of the baby's washcloths, and just *be*. Please let there be peace while this happens—please, no sibling fights, no screams from the crib, no toddlers taking a header down the stairs, no phone calls or doorbells. I left everyone safe and happy, please could they just stay that way until I'm done? Then, I promise, I will emerge like Lazarus from the tomb to be a patient and sweet-tempered mom ready to start her day—with shiny hair to boot. Thank you.

4

TRACY MAYOR

PRAYER
for the Car Seat

♥

Dear God, Is there a reason why this goddamned—excuse me, *blasted*—car seat won't click in? Am I doing something wrong? Aside, of course, from muttering every curse word I know right into my baby's ear as I try to get this thing working. I've been diligent. I did my homework. We spent three weeks and untold hundreds of dollars buying the most perfect seat for our baby, our car, our lifestyle ("comfort foam"—who knew we needed *that*?). I read all fifteen pages of the instruction booklet, I downloaded the Important Consumer Updates. I now know enough to give an impromptu lecture on the benefits of the LATCH system. The harness straps are perfectly adjusted, the baby's sitting at the age-appropriate angle, everything is correct. My kid could hurtle off a cliff in this thing and emerge uninjured, if only the damn buckle would click in. Okay, perhaps there is half a bagel jammed down there, also a few random Goldfish. Please, God, could you just overpower that gunk with your might? Sometimes a little majesty from on high is better than any human engineering, and I'm thinking now is one of those times. Just one zap from you and we're on our way! Thanks, God. I owe you one.

PRAYER
on My Yoga Mat

💙

Dear God, Because I know you cherish each and every one of us as unique individuals of your creation, I just wanted to report that the beautiful body that I used to inhabit is missing in action. If you've seen it in your travels through the universe, I would like it back. Once upon a time, I was that hot yoga chick in the front of the class, moving with great power and precision (also with a great ass, thank you Lululemon Groove Pants) through Mountain, Garland, Forward Fold, Monkey, Plank, Downward-Facing Dog, and on and on. Now I unroll my mat in my toy-strewn family room, inhale deeply, and think *Wow, moldy! I really need to soak this thing in tea tree oil.* Not quite the enlightenment I was after. I lie here, curled up in Child Pose, trying to stretch out a back that's tight and sore from dragging the stupid baby carrier everywhere, and all I can focus on is how ginormous my boobs, belly, thighs, and butt have become. They should call this Child*birth* Pose. Help me to be at peace with the new, larger me while my body does the right thing and loses the baby weight slowly and naturally (nine months on, nine months off). But when the time is right, Lord, could I maybe get that killer ass back? Just asking, and thanks.

PRAYER
for the Stroller

❤

Dear God, Please help me fold this stupid stroller without having to flag down a work crew for help. I know this is a reasonable request, Lord, because I looked at other strollers, *good* strollers, so I know one-handed folding is possible in this world. Remember that first stroller I fell in love with, the one with adjustable swivel-wheel suspension, three-position tilting seat, mosquito net, sun canopy, and aerated mattress inlay, offered in twenty-seven customizable fabrics, including fleece and canvas? The one that cost $899? Or the one used by the Famous Actress that has a five-point harness system, foot-operated linked parking brakes, safety lights, plus clock and thermometer? That one cost only $360 (not including hood, shopping basket, or rain cover). I was good, Lord, you have to admit: I was thrifty. So thrifty that I wound up with a $43.98 stroller from the mega-giant superstore, the one with the ugly monkey fabric. Not only does it *not* have one-handed folding, it seems to have no folding at all. Which means I have to lay my now-screaming baby on the pavement and use both hands *and* both feet to get it to close. So please, Lord, if you could send a little Godly force down upon this infernal item, I would be most grateful. Thanks.

TRACY MAYOR

PRAYER

for Pumping at the Office

●

Dear God, Here I am, huddled in a dusty utility closet, half naked and half deafened by the noise of my top-of-the-line, ultra-expensive double breast pump, which is supposed to be "whisper-quiet," but is not. I'm staring at a picture of my sweet baby girl and working on my relaxation breathing, all in an effort to suck as much breast milk out of me as humanly possible in the fifteen minutes before my next conference call. With the dials turned all the way up to "stun" and both breasts going simultaneously, I'm feeling more cow than human just now, Lord, but I don't want you to think I'm not grateful for my tiny closet. Though I could use a lock on the door—last week, Dave from Sales Support walked in on me, which was extra funny seeing as the poor kid is nearly young enough to remember nursing himself. This pumping business is awkward for everyone, Lord. Please give me the patience and strength to hang in there for the sake of my baby daughter. And please help Dave recover from his embarrassment enough to be able to look me in the eye at next week's meeting. Thanks, God.

PRAYER

for the Perfectly Balanced Toddler Diet

○

Dear God, Would you care for a rice cake topped with peanut butter, grated carrots, and honey? No? How about a cottage-cheese sundae? Perhaps silken tofu with avocado and pear? None for you, thanks? Well, guess what, my toddler feels the same way. She would like to eat Goldfish, graham crackers, Goldfish, banana, Goldfish, hot dogs (the bad kind with nitrates), Goldfish, MultiGrain Cheerios, Goldfish, grilled cheese, and Goldfish. Notice the lack of pureed parsnip, broccoli dippers, or whole-wheat anything. As my own mother keeps saying, "Those green beans would go down better with a little butter and salt." I tell her the rules have changed, but in my heart, I think she's right—is a tiny dab of butter and a few grains of salt really going to set my little girl on the path to morbid obesity? Those "best" toddler diets are like world peace, God—a nice idea but not attainable in our lifetime. Please help my girl to grow up healthy, as active and muscley and athletic as they come. And in the meantime, please don't punish us if we relax a little about what she eats and doesn't eat—including that modern-day manna from heaven, Goldfish. Thank you.

14

PRAYER

When the Phone Rings

❤

Dear God, I don't see a lot of teenagers standing at their mothers' elbows saying, "Me talk, me talk, my turn Mama, my turn" in ever-louder voices, so I'm assuming at some point my son will outgrow his obsession with the phone. Until then, Lord, please, can I have three minutes of peace to conduct a little household business? I'm not even asking for what I truly long for, which is an hour of heart-to-heart with my mom or my sister. No, I just need to call the contractor about our leaking roof, renegotiate our mortgage yet again, and leave messages for all seven members of our playgroup. And I really need to do those things without the background keening and wailing of my little guy. He wasn't fooled by the toy phone, even though it was the electronic kind that looks and sounds exactly like a cell phone. He's not fooled by the old rotary-dial phone we bought him at a yard sale, and he won't let himself get distracted by obvious bribes like cookies or television. I know I need to be careful what I pray for here, Lord: I know one day soon enough he'll morph into a sullen teen who won't so much as grunt hello into the phone. But for now, Lord, could you please consider moving him along to the next developmentally appropriate obsession? Thanks.

PRAYER

for PBS Programming

♥

Dear God, Please let my girl's most favorite PBS show be on right now so I can take a shower. Not the pedantic show where the "Let's get every toddler reading!" slant is obvious even to a three-year-old. Not the one where all the characters' voices are so high and squeaky that the dog hides under the sofa and my daughter gets all crazy-hyper-insane. Not the one with the perfectly balanced cast of multicultural characters that some-how, sadly, manages to be crashingly boring. Not the one that has so many licensed products related to it (Stuffed animals! Puzzles! Software! Blocks! Ride-ons! Liquid gel toothpaste!) that it makes her melt down every time we go shopping. Not *Sesame Street—my* favorite, even after all these years—only because she wanders off whenever Big Bird's onscreen, and I need her to stay put. No, please let this week's current favorite be on, the one with the sweet and earnest round-headed boy (her first crush?) and his mild friends and intact family unit (Mom, Dad, Grandma). And whatever happens, Lord, please do not let it be fund-raising week. We gave, and we'll give again, I promise! But please, God, today let the show be brought to us by the same-old "proud sponsors" and "viewers like you." Because this viewer's Mom really needs a shower. Thanks, God.

PRAYER

at Preschool Pickup

●

Dear God, Please let me be on time. Please help this stupid woman ahead of me in her gigantic planet-trashing SUV turn off her phone and make the left turn already. And then please keep the light green for just one more second. Please don't let me be late, or, if it's somehow your will that I be late, please fill the small, tight heart of the program director with mercy and pity so that she doesn't charge me the completely outrageous one-dollar-per-minute late fee. Please let there not have been any more biting. Please don't let those moms with the perky blond ponytails and the girly pink baseball caps judge my child. Please don't let them give each other that *look*, or at least please don't let me see them do it. Please let my baby be happy today. Please no tears, please not that thing with the screaming and the knees. Please let us have peace at pickup. Thank you. Amen.

PRAYER

at the Park

●

Oh God, Please let my kids behave today. Please let *me* behave today. Please let the line at the slide be orderly—please no pushing or biting. Please stop my girl from giving everyone her Furrowed Brow of Death stare. Please no flinging of sand in the sandbox, please no coveting anyone else's toys (which always seem so superior to ours, no matter how many I bring). Please let at least one baby swing be open so my little guy can hang out there happily. Please let the other infant swings be filled with babies who have normal moms—just for today, God, please no Yummy Mummies with their toned arms and their expensive sunglasses and the cute capris that somehow don't make them look like a stuffed sausage with sawed-off legs, which is what happens when *I* try to wear cute capris. Please no lectures from the Armageddon Moms over the toxicity of my child's pacifier, snack, discount clothing, or stroller manufactured in China. Please let us have a perfect visit today. In return, I promise to keep my mouth shut about politics, feminism, homeschooling, religion, and SpongeBob. Hoping we can work something out, God, and thanks.

PRAYER

for the Simultaneous Nap

Dear God, I know this one is tricky, but you're the go-to guy for miracles, after all. Please let both of my precious children nap this afternoon, and for once in their young lives, let them nap *together* so I can get something done in this house or, God forbid, my life. I've been working hard, literally since dawn, to make this nap happen. I've done all the things they say to make sure the baby's ready for a good nap—given her plenty of infant stimulation, fed her at the right times, kept her from dozing off too early in her carriage, made sure she's in a quiet, darkened place with the correct temperature and humidity. And I've done everything to make my three-year-old ready to conk out as well. If this backfires, Lord, I am totally sunk for the rest of the day—it'll just be me and two screeching, severely overtired kids from now till bedtime. So, please, God, send down your sandman vibes on my little ones. If you can't swing this, nobody can. Thank you.

TRACY MAYOR

PRAYER

before the Grocery Store

Oh God, Please let this be a good and productive shop. Please help me to keep my wits about me, even though I appear to have left my list at home. Please give me the clarity of mind to remember that, like the animals on the ark, good things come in pairs: the peanut butter and the jelly, the bagels and the cream cheese, the yogurt and the 100 percent organic no-fructose no-sat-fat cereal bars, the Fresh Step and the Meow Mix. Please let this not be senior citizen day, or, if it is your will that it be so, please give me patience and good cheer as I maneuver around their carts, which clog every aisle. Please help me to remember that the time will come when I too will need help reaching the extra-large box of All-Bran on the top shelf. Please open my heart so I never forget that this $105 worth of groceries is a blessing and that I should therefore swing by the food bank and deposit some of it on their doorstep. Please give me the time to do this and not be late for preschool pickup. Amen.

PRAYER

at Costco

Dear God, Was this a mistake, bringing my days-old baby to this cavernous warehouse? We needed diapers, the palm-sized newborn diapers with the sweet little cutout for the umbilical stump, and we needed them cheap. And baby wipes by the case. And Advil for Momma's sore you-know-what. And enormous tubes of Desitin. My cart's already halfway full. And yet, Lord, I do feel a little anxious, showing my baby all this *stuff* so early on in her life. Does she really need to know, at nine days old, that Americans are happiest buying their shampoo in fifty-ounce bottles, paper towels by the case, and calcium tablets in massive five-hundred-count jars? On the other hand, the cart is as big as her crib, which makes me feel safe, out with her in public for the first time. And she's mesmerized by the enormous overhead lights. Also, I can't help noticing they've got a special shipment of Italian-milled 100 percent Egyptian cotton sheets, too inexpensive to ignore. God, please help both of us to be grateful for the things that make our lives safe and secure, and remind us to always be thankful for a good bargain. Especially bed-sheets with a high thread count. Thanks.

PRAYER
for the Snowsuit

❤

Dear God, Please help me get this baby into her snowsuit. Please unstick the zipper. Please stop my girl from doing her full-body, arch-backed, stiff-armed, no-snowsuit-no-way maneuver. I admit, maybe it was a little crazy dragging a three-month-old and a three-year-old out into what's been forecast as an all-day blizzard. But hey, fresh air is good for children, right? We bundled up, we jumped out of the way of the plows, we made it to our neighbor's house in one piece, and we had a good long playdate. But now it's time to go home and, God, I could use a little help here. Suddenly it seems easier to summit Mt. Everest than to wrestle two overtired kids into snowsuits, boots, hats, mittens, and neck warmers. The baby in particular, Lord—could you send her some peaceful vibes? It's like trying to put pantyhose on a starfish, she's that wiggly. Oh, one last thing—could you cut back on those thirty-mile-per-hour wind gusts till we get home? I totally owe you, Lord.

TRACY MAYOR

PRAYER

before Swim Class

●

Dear God, Are Baby 'n' Me swim classes strictly necessary for the advancement of humanity? I only ask because it's the unholy hour of 8:30 A.M., and I'm standing here shivering in waist-deep water at our local Y, holding a six-month-old who is not exhibiting the slightest interest in putting so much as a toe into the pool. Please let it be the good teacher this week—the potato-shaped gray-haired lady who somehow seems to know instinctively which babies can be coaxed into the water and which should be left alone. Let it not be the hot-bodied twenty-something instructor who sets all the dads' hearts pounding but actually doesn't know anything about children. Please let that red-headed boy with his red-headed dad not scream the entire forty-five minutes and freak out every other child in the pool, as he did last time. Please let my own little guy stop clinging to me for dear life and at least give the water a try. Please let his swim diaper hold out, as it did not last week, and please let him not hack up half a gallon of pool water in the dressing room, as he also did last week. Most important, please let the next forty-three minutes whiz by so we can get to the part of the morning we both adore: when my guy is eating his cereal-bar snack, wrapped in his adorable doggy towel with the floppy ears and terry tail, and I'm back in dry clothes with my hands wrapped around a double non-fat latte. Thanks, God, and please hurry.

TRACY MAYOR

PRAYER

at the Beach

Dear God, This is not exactly the day we planned. Our baby is naked, utterly caked with sand (it's even hanging from her eyelashes), and screaming bloody murder because we've told her it's time to go. She's had no nap, no snack, none of the peaceful moments at the shore that we imagined. It's laughable that her father and I both brought books to read—what were we thinking? She's swallowed at least a half-gallon of sea water, stomped on every sand castle within a hundred yards of our blanket, stripped off her swim diaper, and peed in front of a large family group from some Scandinavian country (think tiny Speedos and white-white skin). We need to leave before this meltdown gets any worse, Lord, but packing up our ten thousand belongings is going to be a nightmare. We have sand toys, water toys, swim diapers, a jog stroller with all-terrain wheels, a pop-up tent, two beach chairs with cup holders (hey, we're spoiled, what can we say?), sunscreen, an SPF sun shirt size 2T, one of those nerdy hats with flaps, a quick-dry beach sheet, bug spray, a beach umbrella, one cooler with baby snacks and drinks, and a separate Mommy and Daddy cooler. Please, Lord, if you could somehow help us to get from here to our car with our belongings and our sanity intact, I promise next time we're craving a little sun, we'll stay home by the blow-up kiddie pool. Thanks.

PRAYER

for My Unwashed Hair

♥

Dear God, I know I look like holy hell, if you'll pardon the expression. I'd put on a little lipstick if I had any idea where one was—the last tube I used, as you might recall, ended up on the walls of our mudroom. I'd wash my face if this clingy, teething toddler you have blessed me with would let go of my kneecap for even one minute. I'd wash this hideous hair if six moms from playgroup weren't due to pull into our driveway in twenty minutes in their matching SUVs, expecting iced tea and homemade cookies and a family room cleared of choking hazards. So for now, Lord, please bless my greasy locks and give me the power to fluff them into some semblance of a Perky Mom updo. Also, please give me the vision to find a scrunchie in the next thirty seconds. Thank you, Lord, and amen.

PRAYER

for Loading the Diaper in Public

Dear God, Just slay me now, so I don't have to die of embarrassment on my own. Here we are, in church of all places, and my little guy chooses the one music-free moment of the service to load up his diaper. And it's not just one-push-and-we're-done, oh no. He's grunting, he's red-faced, he's gasping, he's writhing in my arms. It's completely obvious to anyone over the age of two what's going on. I'd take him out to the nursery, but this kid's digestive tract is so tetchy, if I move him now, he won't go again for days. The family with four boys behind us has completely dissolved into giggles, but the proper lady on the end of our row is not amused—she's taken out her perfumed hanky, a sure sign of disapproval. Lord, I know everybody poops, I've read that damn book a million times. And I'm not exactly a shy type myself—delivering a couple of babies will cure you of that pretty quickly. Still, this moment is agonizing. I'm afraid the congregation is going to burst into applause when he finally finishes. Please,

Lord, could you start up the music or perform some sort of minor miracle to distract everyone? Causing even one congregant to speak in tongues would help. You might consider the lady with the hanky as a prime candidate. Thanks, God.

PRAYER
for My Smartphone

○

Lord, Is this some kind of cosmic joke? A message from you to me that I've become too attached to my smartphone, that I should "hang up and parent," to borrow the phrase? Because I just found my precious gadget, my lifeline to the world, floating in the cat's water bowl. My daughter was playing with the program that shows the fishies swimming across the screen, and, well, fishies belong in water. Real water. Lord, I know we've become too attached to technology. I know that the best things in life are real people, real relationships, real physicality. But God, that phone does more to keep me sane than you might realize. It gives me perspective; it keeps me balanced; it brings me back to the person I used to be before I had kids. Also, it reminds me that we need peanut butter and Goldfish. Now the phone is soaked, and the screen is displaying nothing but a sickly web of horizontal and vertical lines. I'm trying to revive it with a hair

TRACY MAYOR

dryer, but things aren't looking good. Lord, I know it's a shallow request in a world full of wants, but please revive my smartphone. Or at least save my music library? Thanks.

PRAYER
for My Five-Minute Nap

Dear God, I cannot go on. It is four in the afternoon: My morning caffeine high is long gone, and I have hours and hours to go before I manage to get to bed. I am quite certain I could crash to the floor this instant and sleep like a rock for a week. Please, can I have just five minutes to pass out? I cannot read one more syllable of *Owl Babies,* I can't even lift my hand to turn the page, I am that tired. Please let my chattering little monkey—who is busy telling me each owl baby's name and what they like to do when their mother is gone—please let her not notice that *her* mother is gone. Please let her be oblivious as I quietly lose consciousness. Please, not that thing where she says, "Mommy, pick up your head! Those aren't the right words! Why is your voice funny?" Five minutes, God, and I'll be a new woman, ready to push through the rest of the day. Thank you.

TRACY MAYOR

PRAYER

for My Neighbor Out Sweeping Her Driveway, Again

❤

Dear God, Please give me an open and loving heart, big enough that I can forgive my neighbor's nasty, judgmental demeanor. Please give me the patience to be kind to her as she complains about the Wiffle ball in her flower bed, the noise of the Big Wheel on our driveway, the leaky juice box left in her mailbox by accident. Please give me strength as she tells me again about her well-mannered children, the quiet ones who colored within the lines and stayed inside their fence; who never wandered the neighborhood in pajamas and a cowboy hat, as my kiddo does. Please let us make it through this gloriously sunny afternoon without any tense little comments from her. Please give me the clarity to remember that soon enough, my kids will be grown and gone, as hers are. And when that time comes, Lord, please grant me a nicer disposition than you have given her. Amen.

PRAYER
at McDonald's

●

Dear God, I'm a responsible, eco-aware mama. I read *Animal, Vegetable, Miracle*. I know the dangers of Big Food. So why are we here? Because my kids are starving and I'm exhausted and we're broke, and McDonald's means cheap food and free entertainment for small children. Also, the fries are to die for. That said, we are not even done with ordering, and I'm already regretting it. My kids are hanging on my knees asking for every random thing on the menu. Oh, I know McDonald's is trying to peddle healthier food for kids, it's just—that's not the food my kids want to order. They want to order M&M McFlurries. Which they're not getting. God, I know this is not a healthy choice in the long run, but please just look the other way today as my kids plow through their Happy Meals searching for the toy, gobble down a few fries and a couple bites of chicken nugget, and savor the thrilling experience of running wild through a public space with one hundred other screaming kids. Thanks for cutting us some slack today, God. Also, thanks for creating a world that includes McDonald's fries. They are evidence that miracles truly exist.

prayers for
Sleepless Nights

PRAYER

upon Leaving Work at 5 P.M. on the Dot

❤

Dear God, If looks could kill, I'd be dead now, stabbed in the back by my coworkers, who are throwing stares that say "Who does she think she is?," "Must be nice," and "Sure, I don't mind picking up your slack, go off and bond with your spawn." I *am* going off to bond with my spawn, thanks very much. I cannot wait to bury my face in my sweet babe's chubby neck after this excruciatingly long day. Also, our over-the-top day-care provider charges a buck a minute for any child picked up after 5:30 P.M., so yes, I am out of here. But it's more than that, Lord—something's happened with me and work. It's just not the center of my world anymore. My baby is. I'm working as hard as I ever have, in some ways a lot harder because I'm cramming more day into fewer hours. But I don't have time anymore for lunchtime walks and mid-afternoon coffees and half hours of morning pleasantries, and I'm afraid my childless workmates resent me for that. Lord, please don't let them pick apart my work. Please help them resist the urge to pettily track my hours. And, really, please keep them from throwing those murderous glances my way when the clock clicks to 5 P.M. I can't afford to have anything slow me down. Thanks, God.

PRAYER

for Daddy Coming through the Door

💙

Holy God, What time is it? Is it 6:40 yet? The last time I checked it was only twenty past. Six forty is when my man walks through that door, but Lord, I cannot wait another minute. My girls cannot wait. The baby is washed and changed, ready to sleep and waiting to nurse. She's unbelievably fussy, but she has to see her daddy before bed. Our big girl won't take her bath with anybody but Dad these days, no matter how late he makes it home. She's dancing between the front door and the kitchen, unable to settle on an activity when she knows he's so close. God, I know I can be hard on my husband sometimes. The day is so staggeringly long with two little kids, and he's gone for such a big chunk of it, eleven-something hours with the commute. I know I give him lists of too many things to do from work because I can't, and I call him too many times during the day, or our daughter does, or we e-mail him or IM him or post a video we want him to watch right away. And now, when he walks through that door, we descend on him like a plague of locusts. God, please make sure he knows how much his home-coming means to us. Some nights, the sound of his step on the threshold and the sight of his handsome, tired face is enough to make me cry. Thank you for bringing him home safe to us every night. And when he remembers to bring home diapers and Goldfish like I asked him to, we are all doubly blessed, so thanks two times over.

PRAYER

for Two Working Parents

❤

Dear God, Here is my husband, my soul mate, my life partner, my co-parent. Please do not let me fight with him after this long and difficult day and crappy commute home. Please give me patience when he plunks his briefcase and newspaper smack in the middle of the already cluttered kitchen island, rifles through the mail, and says, "What's for dinner?" as if both of us have not been out of the house since 7:15 this morning. Please give me strength when he ignores the sitter, even though it's her day to be paid, or when he begins chasing the kids through the living room, when he knows full well they're both in desperate need of baths and an early bedtime. Please don't let us nitpick over garbage, dirty socks, unfolded laundry, unanswered messages, unpaid bills, or unattended toilet-seat lids. Please help me remember he's been working hard all day and feels entitled to a little downtime. More important, Lord, please remind him that *I've* been working hard all day too and am entitled to a little downtime. Isn't this why You, in your infinite wisdom, invented Chinese takeout? Thank you for that, Lord, and thanks for keeping the peace in our two-career household. Amen.

PRAYER
before the Freezer

Dear Lord, Please let there be something edible in here. Something I can pop in the microwave for a quick thaw, dump a little sauce over, and call dinner. Maybe even an entrée-like thing *and* a vegetable item—is that too much to ask? I did not make it to the store today (or the post office, or the dry cleaners, or the library). I was having one of *those* days. Now it's dinnertime, and we all could use a decent meal, but I'll be damned if I'm strapping anybody in the car to go back out and get what I need. So please, God, let there be something appealing in one of these frozen lumps of foil. Something not too old, something that won't taste like freezer burn, something nutritious and versatile—kid-friendly and yet still sophisticated enough for the adults. And speaking of adults and bad days, is it wrong to hope that one of those bottles in the very back of this freezer might have a tiny splash of vodka left in it? Either way, thanks for whatever you can rustle up.

PRAYER

for the High Chair

♥

Dear God, I know it's a sin to hate, but it is okay to hate an in-animate object? Because, Lord, I loathe this high chair. I am sick to death of every nook and cranny of this thing, and boy do I know every nook and cranny, thanks to my messy, fussy daugh-ter. Last week I actually dragged it out to the driveway and power-washed it with the garden hose, and it *still* isn't completely clean. What can I say, I have a kid who loves yogurt from the tray, peanut butter off the spoon, cottage cheese, scrambled eggs, peaches, sweet-potato cubes, overripe pears, mashed bananas, and of course that baby staple, rice cereal, which can double as wallpaper paste once it dries. I hate this chair's one-handed, quick-release tray, which is actually neither of those things. You need more tentacles than a squid to yank it free. I hate its nonslip double-thick upholstery and through-the-crotch safety straps, which do indeed keep my daughter safe but also make her feel like a prisoner, which is no way to develop a love of good food. The only thing I hate more is the thought of trying to feed my daughter without this chair. Then the sweet potatoes will be on the tablecloth and the mashed bananas on the walls. So please, Lord, help me find a way to make peace with this odious item, if even for just a few more months. Thank you.

PRAYER

for the Family Dinner

Dear God, I'm sorry, but I cannot eat any more grilled cheese. Or scrambled eggs. Or French toast. I cannot swallow another tofu pup or white-meat chicken nugget or even one mouthful more of "bunny noodles," the organic-mac-and-cheese-with-the-purple-rabbit-on-the-box. I am going mad and getting fat on kid dinners, so please help me, Lord, as I try something really crazy: a family dinner with adult food. That's right, all four of us at the same table (well, one in a booster chair and another in a high chair), eating broiled line-caught halibut with wilted Savoy cabbage and parsnip-potato puree. A crisp sav blanc for the parents; white grape juice for the kids; candles and cloth napkins all around. God, please let us make it through the next twenty minutes without a major meltdown, blowup, or food fight. I know my kids are still really young, but tonight I'm at the end of my culinary rope. I need some sign

TRACY MAYOR

from you, however tiny, that someday sane, adult-style dining will return on a regular basis to my life. Please let this be the night when they actually eat their food, rather than smushing it, mashing it, smearing it, or wearing it. Please let our conversation be punctuated by laughter and wit, not tears or angry epithets ("stupid head" chief among them). Tomorrow, I promise, I'll be back to pancakes for dinner, but just for tonight, let Julia Child, or at least Rachael Ray, reign over our table. Thank you.

PRAYER

for Head-Banging Music Turned Up Loud

❤

Dear God, What? Sorry, I can't hear you. The music's turned up. Way up. Way, way up. The car windows are vibrating, the floor is thumping, and I'm loving it. Today was pure hell, Lord. Stuck in the house by endless rain with a tantruming toddler and a teething infant, and, to top it all off, I just discovered we're out of diapers. Before my husband could even offer, I grabbed the keys and fled to the car. I'm taking the long way around to the mega-giant superstore so I can clear out my crappy karma with a few head-bangers. God, thank you for the Red Hot Chili Peppers and Pearl Jam, Green Day and Foo Fighters, Pixies and Public Enemy, and, going back, Van Halen and Aerosmith and Guns N' Roses. I can't listen to this stuff all the time— heck, I practically never listen to it anymore, too many f-bombs for little ears—but when times get really tough, there's nothing better for beating a bad mood. Now, if you'll excuse me, Lord, I'm one mom who's "Livin' on a Prayer."

TRACY MAYOR

PRAYER

for the Newborn Bath

●

Dear Lord, Are we ever going to get any better at this baby-washing business? It takes twenty minutes to prep for a two-minute bath! You have to warm the room; warm the water and test it over and over (with your elbow, the inside of your wrist, the digital baby-bath thermometer that always seems to be inaccurate); lay out the cute little duckie hoodie towel with its matching lambikins washcloth (gotta use those shower gifts); assemble the organic foaming baby wash and calming botanical baby lotion; and—oh yeah—undress the actual baby, who in our case starts wailing the second he even hears the water run. We've already ditched the top-of-the-line baby tub we bought before he was born—it's a back-breaker. So here we are, propping up our naked baby in the kitchen sink, where he looks not a little bit like a large roaster. He's wriggling and writhing so much I can barely hold on to him, and it doesn't help that our chubby little dumpling has more folds on him than the Michelin Man.

Lord, I know all this takes time. I know someday I'll get good at this, probably just in time for him to graduate to the big tub. In the meantime, please watch over my husband and me as we muddle through these early months. Please let our mistakes be little mistakes and not life-threatening mistakes. Soap in the eye we can live with. Just please protect us from dropping our slippery wet babe on the floor. Thanks, God.

PRAYER

for the Babysitter

⌄

Dear God, Am I doing the right thing, leaving my precious baby with this very young girl? She's almost sixteen, but somehow I imagined her as bigger and more mature. She's tiny and quiet as a mouse, both of which make me nervous, though I couldn't tell you why. I was already dragging my feet about getting showered and changed for our big date night. Now I'm feeling ill with anxiety. She comes as highly recommended as a high-school babysitter can—heck, I practically had to bribe my girlfriend to get her to fork over this girl's name and number. Still, we've never left our precious baby with anyone before, especially not this . . . child. True, the restaurant is so close, we could be home in less than seven minutes if we needed to be, as my husband has now repeated three times—each time just a little less sweetly. So why am I wiping away tears when I should be putting on a coat of mascara? Please help me to relinquish my baby every once in a while to someone else, even this sweet stranger. Help her to stay awake and sober and un-iPodded so she can hear the tiniest peep from the baby monitor. Let me be able to enjoy an evening out with my husband. And please let it all be over with as soon as humanly possible. Thanks, Lord.

PRAYER

for the Blankie

❤

Dear God, No, this is not a dishrag. It's not something the cat dragged in, or something that's going out in tomorrow's trash. It's my child's beloved blankie—or, more technically, the frayed, grayed remains of what was once his blankie. I have to wash it by hand now; it would shred in the machine. It's been sneezed on, peed on, and puked on. We've left it on an airplane (it went on to San Juan without us), left it locked in the preschool cubby over an excruciatingly long weekend, and left it, the day before I delivered Baby No. 2, in the kids' shoe store at the mall. Most days, my Big Boy doesn't need it anymore. But come nighttime, Lord, it's our Secret Sauce, our magic wand, our Mr. Sandman. God, I know the world is a mutable place and that all things must pass, but if you in your infinite wisdom have kept around the duckbill platypus and the horseshoe crab, can't you see fit to keep this nearly transparent square of cloth alive for just a little longer? Someday our son won't need it anymore, which will be a great relief to his father, who's getting worried. Until then, Lord, help him—and me—to stay off the kid's back until he's ready to give it up on his own terms. Help us to remember what that great child-development specialist, Linus, said: Happiness is a thumb and a blanket. Thanks, God.

TRACY MAYOR

PRAYER
for Crying It Out 1

Dear God, Have fifteen minutes gone by yet? I swore I wasn't going to look at the clock. It must be fifteen by now. It's probably closer to half an hour. I'm lying here in the dark, utterly ravaged by exhaustion, listening to our baby cry. And cry. And cry. We've done everything the sleep books say to, Lord—we established healthy daytime nap schedules and comforting nighttime sleep rituals. We left our guy drowsy but not asleep in his crib, and we returned briefly at the proper intervals to soothe him without overstimulating him. No, he's overstimulating himself just fine without any help from us. He's standing rigid in his crib, clutching the bars so hard his tiny knuckles are white, screaming in rage and fear. And he's been like that, I swear to you, Lord, for forty-five minutes. My husband is asleep beside me, which is probably for the best. He's at the end of his rope with both of us. He put his pillows over his head and said he doesn't care if neither of us ever sleeps again, and the way things are going, I feel we never may. I can't stand it, Lord. This isn't working. After all it's been . . . whoa. Nine minutes. *Nine* minutes, that's all? Those were nine long minutes, God. Okay, so maybe I'm an utter wimp, but I'm going in there. Forgive me, Lord, for I have failed to Ferberize.

PRAYER

for Crying It Out II

Dear God, I caved. I couldn't hack it. I allowed my child to cry for exactly nine minutes before I swept in there like an angel from heaven and rescued him. The poor kid—his diaper was half shredded, his entire face was swelled up red like a tomato, snot was pouring down his cheeks, and he had that huh-huh-huh hiccup breathing of the truly distraught. Imagine if I'd left him the full fifteen minutes, Lord! He'd be traumatized for life! How can he grow up to Do Good Works and Be a Model Citizen if he's emotionally impaired? Now he and I are snuggled up together in mommy and daddy's bed, happy as two peas in a pod, trying to stay as quiet as we can so we don't wake daddy up. Because daddy really wants the baby to go to sleep peacefully in his own bed and stay there all night. But we can cross that bridge another night, right, Lord? Please tell me we can start again when we're both ready? I want to do what's right, just not tonight. Please take pity on us, God, for we have failed to Ferberize.

PRAYER

for Roughhousing

💙

Dear God, I've left the room. I'm hiding in the kitchen. My husband and my daughter—my precious bundle with the soft bones and the still-developing neck muscles—are in the other room roughhousing. I would like to tell you she's whimpering with fear and he's stopped what he's doing and is comforting her responsibly. But the fact is he's tossing her through the air with utter disregard for even rudimentary safety considerations, and she is squealing with unfettered joy. How did a woman like me, a safe, cautious, rule-following, let's-not-die-needlessly person, give birth to such a little daredevil? She's a climber and a jumper and a let's-play-airplane type, but mostly she's a girl who knows how to push her father's buttons. He zooms, she screams, he does it again, she screams louder. They play Superman, airplane, piggyback, Baby Upside Down, and daddy tiger/baby tiger, and all I can think of is dislocated shoulders, detached retinas, and whiplash. Lord, I realize there are times to speak up and times to shut up. Help me be strong enough to step out of the way and let the two people I love most in the world go at it without me. Help me to trust my husband to be careful with his daughter. Keep our daughter safe as she goes through life, but also help her keep her wonderful sense of adventure and bravado. It's great for her, and it's great for her dad. Even if it's killing me. Thanks, Lord.

PRAYER

for *Goodnight Moon*

○

Dear God, In the great green room, there was a telephone, and a red balloon, and a picture of the cow jumping over the moon. Do you want me to go on? Because I can. The bears . . . the chairs . . . the kittens . . . the mittens. I know the entire book by heart, God. I've read it to my kids over and over and over again. I could draw you a picture of every page, showing the tiny differences in that green room from page to page as darkness settles in. The quiet old lady? I want to *be* that lady. My little girl wants to *be* that bunny, to be put to bed in crisp blue-striped pajamas. Thank you, God, that there are children's books like *Goodnight Moon* out there. We have so many bad children's books—mostly gifts, I'm sorry to say—that it makes us treasure our good books so much more. We're tired of books with icky, obvious rhymes, or sparkles or rainbows or holograms or, worse, batteries. We don't like to read books that are really morality tales for adults, or books about self-esteem that tell you they're about self-esteem, or books that try to make kids do something, like poop or go to bed or believe in You. We don't need those books, God, because we have *Goodnight Moon*. This is our nighttime prayer, and it's as full of reverence and praise as they come: *Goodnight stars. Goodnight air. Goodnight noises everywhere.*

PRAYER
before the Dryer

●

Dear Lord, Please let there be some clean clothes in here. I *think* I remember heaving in a load wet from the washer hours and hours ago, when this hellishly long day first began. Now it's close to midnight, and I'm praying I had the presence of mind to wash and dry the baby's most precious blankie so he can soothe himself back to sleep before the sun comes up. Also please let my girl's favorite sparkle skirt be in there too, so she'll go happily off to day care tomorrow without a screaming fit. And boxers—any chance for just one pair for my husband? The poor guy hasn't had clean clothes in days now. If it makes me seem less demanding, Lord, you'll notice I haven't asked for anything for me. Every morning I pull on my same old yoga pants and hoodie, grabbed off the floor where I dropped them the night before. It's disgusting, but hey—cuts down on wash, and it's good for the environment too, right? So please Lord, take pity on my domestic disorganization and serve up some clean and fluffy goodness from this dryer, so the rest of my family doesn't look as grody as their mama does.

PRAYER

for a Girls' Night Out

Dear God, I cannot wait to escape from Mommyland and just go have some fun with my girlfriends tonight. We've spent so long trying to schedule this girls' night out, please let everything be cool. Please stop M. from doing that competitive thing she does, where she has to top anything that anyone else says. We already know her children are more advanced, her husband sexier, and her house more perfect. Please give her peace tonight. Please let L. be happy too, please let her talk about anything else except her husband. We don't want to hear any more about his failings in bed, poor guy. Please rein in S., Lord, you know what she's like on Appletini No. 3. Please let the reins *out* on N., so she can relax and eat a normal-sized meal for once without obsessively counting every calorie and making the rest of us feel fat. And please let me not be a crashing bore, Lord, who has nothing to talk about but my children. They take up so much of my life now—and my entire brain—that sometimes I'm

TRACY MAYOR

afraid there's nothing else to me anymore. Please let the old me come out tonight. These are my best girls in the world, and for all their faults, I love every one of them. Let it be fun like the old days, when we yapped about good shoes and bad boyfriends and worse bosses and hopes and dreams. If I can do all that, drink a horny toad margarita that somehow manages to have no calories, and still be home in bed by eleven, I'd be grateful, Lord. Thank you.

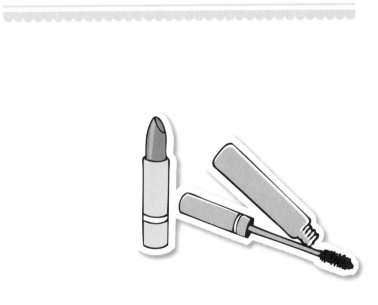

PRAYER

for Facebook

❤

Dear God, I'm logging off. I'm just checking for one more thing, then I'm shutting the computer down and going to bed—it's way after eleven. I just need to see if my girlfriend posted the photos from the preschool pageant—oh, she did! And they came out great! Gotta share these. There, *now* I can log off. Thank you for Facebook, Lord, it's a total lifeline. In one place I can connect with all my local mommy friends, keep up with my friends from college who are raising their kids halfway across the world, stay buddies with a couple of exes (it's all innocent, God, you know that!), and follow the exploits of pretty much everyone from high school without having to actually attend any reunions. It makes me feel less isolated when I see that a friend is having an even worse time with her toddler than I am. (Though from her photo, I see she managed to lose all her baby weight and get fabulous new highlights while she's struggling.) It's good for my brain to be able to keep up with my old coworkers. (Though it's obvious from the technical detail in their wall posts that I'll have a lot of catching up to do when I try to rejoin the workforce.) And, what the heck, it's a good mental-health break to take a quiz about '80s music, or my favorite slasher movies, or 25 Things I Don't Know about My Best Friend. Lord, please help me to tap the good in Facebook without getting sucked into what's mindless or undermining. Help me to be happy for my friends, and help them be happy for me. Help me not to judge—or be judged—too harshly. Most of all, God, please help me to log off when I should. Like now. I promise I'm logging off now. Right after I take this quiz, What Kind of Online Mommy Are You?

PRAYER

before Sex

●

Oh, God, Please let this be fast. But not, you know, *too* fast. Please let it be just enough for both of us, if you get my meaning. Please let our blessed babies stay where they belong, especially Mr. I-just-turned-two-watch-me-climb-out-of-my-crib. Please let me forget about the groceries and that nightmare at pickup this afternoon. Please help me relax. Please send us a little lightning bolt of that old giddy feeling, that wave of engulfing joy that first brought us together, that helped us make this family. Please let us be carried away for just a few minutes. And afterward, please send us sweet release so we sleep in each other's arms like the sheeted dead. It's been, as you know, Lord, a long day. Amen.

74

PRAYER

for No Sex

♥

Oh, God, Please not tonight. Actually, please not for many nights. I just can't, not now. Not when I've been nursing this baby every two hours all day and all night. Also there is the problem with the stitches. Please, Lord, give my man the insight to understand even just a little bit what it feels like to breastfeed—I'm all touched out! I feel like a cow! Please give him the patience to wait. Please let him trust me that we'll get back to where we used to be. I'll be his hot mama, I promise. I *want* to do it, and I want to do it with *him*—heck, we made this baby together, didn't we? And we'll make more, I hope. Just . . . not yet. Please help him to get through this without being angry or sad or distant. Also without having an affair. Thank you, God.

PRAYER

for Breathing

❤

Dear God, I know I'm out of control. I haven't slept more than two hours since I gave birth three weeks ago. Oh, the *baby's* sleeping fine, it's me who can't let go. I know I'm being irrational, but I'm obsessed with the thought that my little girl is going to stop breathing any second. Look at her nose, Lord, adorable, isn't it? But also clearly too small to sustain a breath. Her little bow mouth—so precious and so feminine—just isn't practical for getting enough air into her. Her lungs must be the size of a butterfly's wing, her heart is like a hummingbird's. So I sit here, hour after hour while she sleeps, watching her chest and its impossibly slight ups and downs. I have to admit, God, the package is tiny, but so far it's worked perfectly. It's just . . . will it still work perfectly if I crawl back to my own bed for half a night's sleep? I'm losing it, God. I need to hand off the controls to you and go off-duty for a few hours. Please keep my tiny girl's miniature mechanics working in tip-top shape while I'm gone. You're the man, Lord—please keep those lungs pumping. Thank you.

76

TRACY MAYOR

PRAYER

before Dawn

⌄

Oh, God, Please do not let that be the baby. How can that possibly be the baby? I can't see the clock without my contacts—is it 6:23 in the morning? Could that possibly be a 5, it's *5:23 A.M.*? How can this be? She just nursed an hour ago! Please, Lord, show her mother some mercy, let her find her thumb, send her back to sleep for an hour. Or twenty minutes, God, I will take twenty minutes. Just please, don't make me have to stagger through the day with this little sleep. Thank you. Amen.

prayers for
Meltdown Moments
and Other
Stressful Situations

PRAYER

before the Home Pregnancy Kit 1

●

Oh, God, Please let me be pregnant. Please make the little test strip turn blue. Please let me have another child. You know how much I want this baby, you know how hard I've worked, the tests and the doctors' appointments, and the fertility charts, and those painful injections in the butt every morning. Please make this one stick. Lord, I know it's greedy to ask for another child when I am already so blessed, but other people are blessed too! Please don't let me want to kill myself when I pass one of those triplet strollers filled with beautiful babies. Please let me not be jealous, or grievous, or murderous, when yet another girl-friend tells me her "news." Please give me the patience to wait my turn and the hope to know another turn is coming for me. And maybe could that turn be now—right now? My three minutes is up. The test is ready. Please, God, please let it be a yes. Amen.

PRAYER

before the Home Pregnancy Kit

Oh, God, Please don't let me be pregnant. Please make this test negative. Please do not give me another baby right now. I am so thankful, I am blessed, I love the life you have trusted me with so much, but please, not more, not now. It's all just too much already—the tantrums and the spit-up and the potty seat and the damp laundry going moldy in the dryer. My job, his job, my parents, his parents, the jeans that I still can't get into from last time, the rear brake pads on the minivan about to go and no way to pay for them. Please let this one pass me by. I promise I'll be more careful next time. I promise *he'll* be more careful next time. I promise we won't take so lightly this great gift you have given us. My three minutes is up. The test is ready. Please, God, please let it be a no. Amen.

TRACY MAYOR

PRAYER

for My First Day Back to Work

●

Dear God, No I'm not crying at my desk, how could you think such a thing? It's allergy season, as you know. I just dropped off my baby—my tiny, cherished, weeks-old, still-nursing, so-beloved infant son, our firstborn—at the excellent, state-regulated, well-recommended, hard-to-get-into, super-expensive day-care center close to my office and our home. I have sausaged myself into that old blue pantsuit left over from my "fat days"; my bag is packed with my brand-new, still-uncomfortable, incredibly noisy breast pump; and the electronic picture frame my co-workers gave me at my baby shower is up and running a continuous loop of 237 pictures of my little boy. I'm checking e-mails (900-something since I last logged in) and prepping for the weekly 10 A.M. Monday conference call. A working mother, God, totally on top of her game, that's me. And look, it's already 9:05. Only 475 minutes left in the workday. If I

could task you with just one action item, Lord, could you somehow make me emotionally numb from now till then so I don't
crumble and spend the rest of the morning weeping quietly in
the ladies' room? If you could get on that ASAP, I'd be appre-
ciative.

PRAYER

Five Days Postpartum

Dear God, Everything's going great. Our baby is here and she's perfect. I got through labor the way I wanted to—no epidural!—and I'm proud of myself. The nursing is getting better every day; my husband seems genuinely thrilled with parenthood; and our little peanut is sleeping four hours a stretch at night, which everyone tells us is awesome. So, God, maybe you could tell me: Why do I want to crawl under the covers and cry until I pass out? I'm so happy, and yet—I want my breasts to stop leaking. I want my stitches to stop throbbing. I want this brown sludge to stop bleeding out of me. And most of all, I want my baby, the world's most perfect creature, out of my arms, off my breasts, and back into my womb where she belongs. The two of us were a great team for the last nine months. Why'd everything have to go and change? Lord, some distant part of my brain realizes I'm in the throes of the massive hormone drop that comes post-partum, when it's perfectly normal to feel completely abnormal.

Please let this be a one- or two-day problem, not the beginning of something bigger and deeper. I love my baby, and I love being a mother, but I'm also mourning my old life and my old body. Please let me be able, eventually, to sort out all these feelings and go back to being happy. In the meantime, if you need me, I'll be in bed under a pile of pillows. Thanks, God.

PRAYER
for Colic

Ⓥ

Dear God, Have I offended you? I know I can be smug, what with my great husband, delightful toddler, and happy second pregnancy. Did I get too complacent or ungrateful? Because my new baby has colic, Lord, and at times it's so awful that it feels like nothing but a punishment from a vengeful God. Look at how my child is suffering! In a single day our happy, sleepy newborn turned into a howling, red-faced monster, and no matter what we try, we can't get him back. They say he's not in pain, God, but I'm not a fool. I can see with my eyes and feel with my heart that he's hurting. He's writhing and gasping and emitting that unmistakably ear-splitting colic cry for hours and hours on end. His big sister is angry and clingy and teary, and why shouldn't she be when there's not a moment of peace in the house from three in the afternoon till midnight, every single night? We've been to the pediatrician more times than I can count, and to every specialist in town. We've tried every feeding, holding, sleeping, and soothing trick in the book. I am clinging to the hope that this colic will very shortly end the same way it began—suddenly and without warning. Until then, Lord, please send us the strength and patience to somehow survive through these minutes and hours and days and weeks. You're our only hope, Lord. Thanks.

PRAYER

before the Meltdown

♥

Oh, God, I see this coming like white on rice. I can sense it in my bones the way a small animal knows an earthquake is imminent. But please, God, not here, not now. I know I've pushed my little guy too far all day long—my bad!—but please, do not let him melt down in lane 7 of the mega-giant superstore checkout at 5:43 on a crowded weekday night. Please not in front of High-Heeled Single Gal in her pencil skirts with her Lean Cuisine and pomegranate juice. Please not in front of Crunchy Earth Mama with her wheat-free organic cart of goodness and her three perfectly placid children. Look, Lord, I know it's wrong to force-feed Skittles to a child who can barely chew, but please, I'm trying to buy us five minutes. Please just let us make it to the parking lot before all hell breaks loose. Thank you, and hurry.

PRAYER
after the Meltdown

♥

So, God, Are you there? Could you send me a sign? Just some little signal that it won't always be this bad, that I'm not the worst mother in the world? This meltdown was a full-on nightmare— he screamed, he kicked, he bit, he yelled "No love mommy!" loud enough for the entire mega-giant superstore parking lot to hear. And I did all the bad mommy things I am so judgmental about in other women—the snarl, the hissed threats in his small pink shell of an ear, the shoving him into his car seat like he was a sack of flour. How is it possible to love someone so fiercely and want him, just for a nanosecond, so gone? Now both of us are here, buckled in and crying, too sad and shaken to make it home. Please give me that little jolt of energy to get us out of this parking lot. Please let him forgive me. Please let him forget this. Please let *me* forget this. And really, really: Please let this be the calm at the end of the storm, not the calm at the *center* of the storm. No more meltdowns, not today. Thanks, God.

TRACY MAYOR

PRAYER

for the Letdown of Milk

❤

Oh, Lord, Please help my milk to let down. My breasts are the size of two watermelons, rock hard, and so full I swear my skin is going to rip. Remind me which part of this is "natural" and "beautiful" and "womanly"? Please let the baby—my poor, hungry, days-old infant—stop crying long enough for me to football-hold her into position, with the help, of course, of the fifty-eight-dollar organic cotton nursing pillow, the lactation consultant, my husband-who-might-be-abandoning-us-at-any-second, and my mother, who really should not utter the phrase "You just need to relax" even one more time. Speaking of relaxing, I drank the full sixteen ounces of water, snuck the two ounces of beer, snorted the hormonal nasal spray, took a hot shower, meditated, and cried, and still my milk—gallons and gallons, it feels like— is up *there* and my baby is down *here*, screaming in my lap and starving. Please send us some let-down vibes to get us unstuck from this supply-and-demand problem. Thank you, God.

PRAYER
for My Bottle-fed Baby

Dear God, Please don't let my baby grow up to be an overweight, emotionally stunted loser because I fed him with a bottle. I am a well-informed mother, I read all the literature—twice!—and I know Breast Is Best. But Lord, can't you make it so the bottle is a Very Close Second Best? You saw how hard I tried, you saw how hard *he* tried, poor little mite. He's only sixteen days old. You saw how the breast-feeding thing just doesn't work for us. Please, Lord, can you cut us a little slack? Bless this Similac and make it almost as good? I swear to you, I won't break any other parenting rules—I solemnly vow never to use anything but cloth diapers, never to let anything but organic goodness pass my baby's lips, never to let him watch commercial television when he gets older—just please, Lord, give us a pass on the bottle. Amen.

TRACY MAYOR

PRAYER
for Our Dog, Displaced

●

Dear God, Am I a nutcase? I've just brought home a new, perfect baby—a life-altering milestone in my life and my marriage—and all I can think about is my dog! Where is my pup, my beloved hound, my stinky-breath, wet-nosed, clicky-nailed fur ball? We did exactly what they told us to: I sat with the baby swaddled on my lap, and we let the dog sniff him all she wanted. Then my husband took the baby away, and I gave her lots of snuggles and belly rubs, just like in the old days. So far, so good. But now she's slunk off somewhere, which is not like her, and I'm so distracted I can hardly think of the nursing and diapering and sitz-bathing I'm supposed to be doing. This dog was our first baby! How can I not worry about her? Lord, I know these next weeks and months will be hard on her. Please bless our doggie and keep her the mellow hound she's always been. Please let her not be jealous or aggressive. Please let her love and protect her new baby brother the way she's always loved and protected us. And please help me find time, however busy I am, to give my girl the attention she deserves. She was the first love I shared with my husband. Without that practice, I swear we never would have dared to have a child. Help us to remember that, Lord. Also, that her nails need cutting. Thanks, God.

PRAYER

for the Diaper Left On Too Long

Dear Lord, Please forgive me, for I have been a bad mother. Or at the very least a mother who literally has not had three minutes in her day to tend to the bottom of her youngest child. And now he stands before me, a living, breathing chastisement, wearing what has to be the world's biggest, soggiest Huggie dangling between his legs, clinging onto his little hips with the tiniest possible remaining piece of adhesive tab. Experience tells me this puppy's gonna blow any second, and only You know how bad it could be underneath. Please, God, I already feel so guilty, please no hideous diaper rash already blooming, please no you-know-what so caked-on that it requires a full-body bath, please not that thing where the sinister-looking crystals explode out of the diaper all over his skin, the changing table, and my forearms. I promise to be better, Lord. I promise to find time in our day to take care of my littlest guy's heinie. Just please don't let this diaper be as bad as it looks from here. Thank you.

PRAYER
for Spit-Up

♥

Dear God, Stand back, here it comes. The white river of doom, the voluminous geyser of goo is about to project forth from my offspring. It's like a magic trick—if he takes in five ounces, he'll give me back eight. His poor chin and neck are chapped and raw, and most of the time he smells like sour milk, even with two or three baths a day. His clothes are ruined—all those brand-new brilliant-white onesies and adorable little T-shirts we received as shower gifts? They're all stained various shades of yellow and gray. And let's not even talk about my clothes. Every shoulder of every suit coat, sweater, blouse, and henley is permanently crusted with spit-up. I know I should be grateful, Lord, that things aren't worse than this. I know there are babies in real pain, babies with serious gastro problems, and I'm so happy my little guy isn't one of those. Still, I want to cry when we're out in public and he lets go with a big one. People literally jump back.

TRACY MAYOR

Little kids actually point and scream, *"Ewwwwww!"* God, I know this is a temporary problem. Every expert out there says he'll grow out of it. Lord, could you make that day be soon? I'm running out of patience. And clean shirts. Thanks.

PRAYER

on the Fifth Day of Rain

Dear God, Is this some kind of second coming, some Noah's Ark II? Because otherwise I cannot fathom the need for five days in a row of this pouring, pounding, freezing rain. You know me, God, I am out there in all kinds of weather with my kids—snow, mud, spring showers, sticky hot summer days. But this rain is a whole other kettle of fish, if you'll pardon the pun. Everything we own is soaked, including the stroller, the car seat, and the inside of everyone's rain boots. The baby's Synchilla hoodie smells like a wet dog, and I won't tell you what the dog smells like. Please let up the rain, even just a little bit. We're done with being inside—I cannot make another thing with Play-Doh, build any more forts with the couch cushions, or play any more games of Hi Ho! Cherry-O. Give us a break, God. Just a little sun? Please? Also, while you're at it, a nice dry breeze would help with the moldy boots. Thank you.

TRACY MAYOR

PRAYER

for My Head-Banging Toddler

Dear Lord, Look at this child's face. Can you see what's happened to the perfect infant you gave us? He's grown into a sputtering ball of toddler rage who smacks his forehead on the ground at the slightest upset—today it was the Duplos that wouldn't come unstuck. People look at me as if I'm an abusive mother—and who can blame them, seeing his poor bruised head and his puffy eyes? I understand that this is a preverbal behavior that will go away once my little guy is able to express his feelings better. (Though was it really helpful for the nurse to suggest we put him in a helmet until then?) Lord, please make this phase be over with sooner rather than later. And next time, maybe, could you give us one of those toddlers who holds her breath until she passes out instead? At least that's quiet. And no blood is involved. Thanks, God.

PRAYER
for My Little Wanderer

♥

Dear Lord, Please help me to stop losing my child. Is it me? Is it him? Is it *you*—are you secretly signaling that I'm overprotective and that I need to let him go? Because ever since he was born, all my guy does is try to leave. Remember that time I put him down on the carpet and he rolled under the couch in the few seconds it took me to grab his pacifier from the kitchen? Or the time he managed to get his activity jumper wedged behind the door to the laundry room, even though the thing is guaranteed not to move more than three inches in any one direction? And now today—one minute he's playing quietly in the grass an arm's length away from me, and the next, he's gone. I turned my back for literally thirty seconds, and off he went, across the lawn and down the sidewalk, dressed only in a diaper, thank you very much. And yes, Lord, thanks for arranging to have a judgmental older woman drive by, cell phone in hand, all ready to dial 911. Sheesh, lady, it only *looked* like a half-

100

naked toddler with no mommy in sight. In reality, God, I'm here for my son. You know that, right? Please keep him close to me, at least till he's, say, two or three. And please help me remember that, unlike other mothers with normal children, I truly cannot take my eye off my little bugger, not even for a nanosecond.

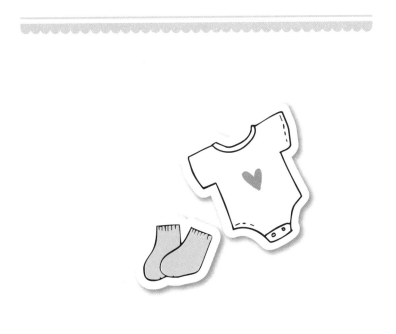

PRAYER
for the Hamster

Oh, God, Please do not let the hamster be dead. Please not right now. I understand that all your creatures, great and small, have their time on earth and then their time to go. But I cannot think of a worse moment for Chunkie to kick the bucket. We are literally on our way out the door to Nana's for the Big Weekend, the one where Mommy and Daddy get to leave the kids behind and act like adults for two whole days and nights. The car is packed; the kids are buckled in. I dashed back into the house just to grab the baby's binky, only to catch a glimpse of Chunkie, lying on his side with one pretty stiff-looking paw poking out. I admit things don't seem great on the health front—that's just not a pose we've seen in the two years we've watched him frolic in his neon-pink Habitrail. Please, Lord, is there any way you could kickstart his little heart? If not, any way we could stave off the decomposition process, just till we get back? Thanks, God, and sorry about the rush.

PRAYER

for the Potty Seat

Dear Lord, Am I the only mother in the history of humanity whose child carries his potty seat literally everywhere, but refuses to actually *poop* in it? He'll sit on it for hours—heck, he even watches TV from there, like it's his little Barcalounger with a splash guard—he just doesn't actually do his business on it. We've scheduled regular bathroom breaks, we've offered cool training pants (Spider-Man) and instant incentives (M&Ms), and we've read *Everybody Poops* ten thousand times and counting. In my heart, I know it will happen sooner or later. It's just, my patience might not hold out that long. The stealth is starting to get to me, Lord—smuggling the potty all over town and hiding his pull-ups from his toilet-trained friends (and their judgmental mothers). We're ready, Lord, we're ready for the next step. If you could give my beloved son's little heinie a heavenly push in the right direction (down into that little plastic bowl), I'd be grateful. Thanks, God.

PRAYER
for My Shy Child

●

Dear Lord, Is this one of your little life lessons, a bit of heavenly irony? You give a loud-mouthed extrovert like me the shyest daughter in the history of preschool? Other kids aren't staring at the toe of their shoe, thumb in mouth, hanging on to their Mama's knees for dear life. Only my little shrinking violet. She's so considerate and cautious, such a peaceful, deep-thinking little soul. God knows the world could use more people like her, Lord. And yet, those aren't exactly traits that play well on the playground. Please remind me that shyness isn't something I need to "fix." Please help me to remember that this isn't anything she chooses, it's not something I can push her to work through. Because I'm not going to lie, Lord, when I see my girl standing there, all alone outside the circle while everyone else is happily playing Wonder Ball, it's like a knife to my heart. Especially then, God, help me to remember that the kids outside the circle in preschool can grow up to be adults who think outside the box, and that's all good. Please help me to honor this shyness as an essential part of who my daughter is. But if it turns out that shyness is something she's destined to outgrow, that's good too—and if that's the case, as always, sooner would be better. Thanks, God.

PRAYER
for My Wild Child

●

Dear Lord, Is this one of your little life lessons, a bit of heavenly irony? You give a reserved, nervous Mama like me the rowdiest kid in the history of preschool? Other boys aren't scaling the playground's chain-link fence half naked, waving their T-shirts over their heads even though it's February. Only my little caveman. In a lot of ways, the world could use more people like him, Lord, intense and persistent. And yet, those aren't exactly traits that play well on the playground. Please remind me that this wildness isn't something I need to "fix," just channel. Please help me to remember this isn't anything he chooses. He's not doing this to be naughty or make his mother insane. Because I'm not going to lie, Lord, when it's time for pickup and I'm pulled aside yet again to be presented with a long list of my guy's transgressions of the day, it's hard not to feel ashamed. And angry. Especially then, God, help me to remember that the kids throwing mud bombs on the playground can grow up to be adults who get things done, and that's all good. Please help me to honor this energy as an essential part of who my son is. But if it turns out that this wildness is something he's destined to outgrow, that's good too—and if that's the case, as always, sooner would be better. Thanks, God.

PRAYER

for Gum from the Ground

❤

Dear God, Help. I am 100 percent skeeved out. While I was talking with my neighbor for two nanoseconds, my child climbed off his new tricycle-with-the-push-bar, pulled a piece of chewed gum off the sidewalk, and popped it into his mouth. You know how I feel about germs, Lord. You know what I was like when I was pregnant. Nine months without setting foot in a movie theater, subway car, or crowded restaurant—well worth the precaution, to my mind. After I delivered, I made it thirty-six months keeping my precious baby boy inside my cleanliness comfort zone—thank you for creating baby wipes, Lord, and thank you for selling them by the case—but all of a sudden the Terrible Twos have hit with a vengeance, and we're off-the-charts grimy here. Gum from the sidewalk, a raisin extracted from his own nasal cavity, the Duplo down his diaper that he nonchalantly retrieved and kept building with . . . so many germs, so little time to follow him around with antibacterial spray. I see other mothers barely blinking as their kids put their filthy hands in their grubby mouths and wipe their snotty noses on their frayed sleeves. Please let me be more like them. (Well, maybe not—that's just disgusting.) Please help me to let go, but not too far. In the meantime, if you need us, we'll be at home, gargling with Listerine. Thanks.

PRAYER

for New Jeans

●

Dear God, Wow, I can't believe I used to pay this much money for denim. I've only been off the fashion market for nine months of pregnancy plus five of recovery, but looking at these clothes, I feel like a sister from another planet. Two hundred and eleven dollars for jeans that I can only wear with three-inch heels? That's not going to happen. I haven't worn anything higher than a clog since the baby was born. Nevertheless, Lord, here I am in the store, out without the baby, looking to fit into some normal clothes—or "new normal," I guess I should say. Please bless my little shopping trip by shutting off the voices in my head, the ones saying "fat" and "flabby" and "no-waist monster butt." Please help me to love and honor this new body—which created a life, after all!—with jeans that won't break the bank or my self-esteem. Send me a sign, Lord: Somewhere in these racks there's got to be a decent pair of stretch dark-wash boot-cuts high enough to hold in this new belly but low enough to make me still look hot. Something that flatters this new "curvy" butt enough to make my husband think I'm sexy without actually making him want sex (or not too often, anyhow). Please show me a jean that won't rip out in the knees, because suddenly I'm on my knees a lot these days, God, crawling after my little guy. Finally, God, if you could locate that perfect jean on the sale rack? That would truly be a miracle. Thank you.

PRAYER

in the Family Restaurant

❤

Dear God, How far the mighty have fallen, no? My dearest partner and I are a long way from our foodie days, when Friday nights meant cozying at the bar with a single-malt scotch, waiting for our wild striped bass and barbecued squab to be plated. Now we're crammed into a four-top table in the smack center of a packed Chain Restaurant (no booths for babies in their carriers, sorry), facing down a decidedly un-gourmet choice of menu items. I'll just have what my toddler's having—the ubiquitous chicken nuggets (what did children eat before the 1980s?), backed up by the omnipresent French fries and the enveloping lake of ketchup, with a few baby carrots tossed in there to appease the health-conscious mothers. Lord, I trust that fancy dinners shall return to our lives at some point (well, maybe not till after college is paid for). In the meantime, let me be content to be here with my beloved and our two kids. Let me be thankful that they're not (yet) spilling their lemonades or pitching their pudding cups, as some of their peers at other tables are. Thank you that we have the money to indulge even this little bit, Lord. And thank you for French fries, which taste great wherever you eat them.

PRAYER

in the Fancy Restaurant

❤

Dear God, What were we thinking? We snuck in super-early to our favorite upscale *enoteca* with our two kids in tow, trying to capture a little bit of that old Friday night magic. But it's been so long since we've been anywhere nice that we forgot a couple of things. For one, Zagat-rated restaurants tend not to have high chairs, kids' menus, or free crayons. For another, there's a lot of *stuff* on the table: wineglasses and water glasses and six or seven pieces of silverware, candles and napkins and fresh flowers, and little tiny bowls of sea salt, all of which could be up-ended with one short, sharp tug of the tablecloth that the baby is currently chewing on. Third, there are not a lot of things on the menu for a child to eat. Lord, please give my picky eaters the courage to at least try what we ordered for them: pasta with butter and cheese, bread, carrots, and strawberries. True, the butter is herbed, the cheese is from Sardinia rather than from the green plastic shaker can that they're used to, the bread has

TRACY MAYOR

caraway seeds in it, and the strawberries are marinated in balsamic vinegar and black pepper. Lord, please let my little ones be so distracted by the oddness of it all that they don't pitch a fit in the middle of this oh-so-proper dining room. Please let us get out of here in the nick of time before they melt down entirely. In exchange, we promise from now on it's back to the Chain Restaurant in the mall for us. Thanks, Lord.

PRAYER

for My Baby Walking Early

○

Dear God, Not to be picky but the baby books say my child should still be three months away on average from taking her first steps—so why is she hell-bent and determined to walk now? I wouldn't mind, except she hasn't got a lick of sense or a modicum of control. Staggering around on her stick-skinny little legs, she looks more like a chicken walking upright than a toddler. She's covered with bumps, bruises, and scrapes, and we've already logged in a black eye and a split lip. My back is killing me from walking bent over behind her, trying to provide some support, which only infuriates her. She wants to walk *now*, damnit, and she wants to walk alone. Last week she took a nasty header down the hill at the playground. Lord, please don't let this be a harbinger of things to come. I don't want my daughter to be one of those kids—or adults—who is always leaping first and looking later. Of course I want my little girl to excel in this world, but not at the expense of her physical safety, or my sanity. Please give her peace to take life as it comes and not rush head-long through every stage of development. God, you've given my girl courage, that we can see. Now could you please mix that with just a dollop of caution? Thank you.

PRAYER

for a Time-Out

❤

Dear God, Help. We have three minutes left on this five-minute time-out, and every second is slashing at my soul. I swear, I'm not going to make it without your help, Lord. My son is sitting on the bottom stair step, banging his head in rage against the banister and howling in pure fury. Why do those stupid discipline books make it sound so easy? Your child breaks a rule, you discipline him coolly and effectively, and poof—he grows up to be a collected, self-possessed adult. Here in the real world, nothing is clear-cut. Yes, my three-year-old bit his baby sister, hard and on purpose. Time-out, no question. But in *his* eyes, he was justified—she "bit" him first with her gummy little baby jaw. Hence his rage. Lord, please remind me it's not always like this. We have days of such joy, days of such sunny silliness, days of peace and play. Today was not any of those days. And now my son is weeping on the steps as if his heart will break, and that's enough for me. Lord, forgive me, but I can't take it for the full five minutes, and neither can my poor, tired son. I know you won't mind if we take a time-out from time-outs. Thanks for understanding, God. I knew you would.

prayers for
Special Days and Special People

PRAYER

for My Maternity Leave 1

❤

Dear God, Is nine weeks of maternity leave really necessary? Don't get me wrong. I adore my baby and am ecstatic to finally be a mom, and I am so grateful that my employers are among the few who give a good maternity package. So thank you for all that. But you know me, Lord, I'm a crazy woman about work. It's just part of my DNA, and not even nine months of pregnancy has rewired that part of my brain. They said, "Don't even think of checking your e-mail," but I couldn't resist—I have gone in and cleaned out my in-box a few times. They said, "Don't give a thought to the next fiscal quarter," but I have jotted down a couple of strategies for goosing revenue. They said, "Just relax and enjoy this time with your baby," and I am, God, I truly am. But just between the two of us, I'm also going to enjoy getting back to work when the time comes. I've found a great nanny and a great backup babysitter, I've pumped and banked my breast milk, and I've bonded thoroughly with my little guy. I know I won't feel guilty when the time comes, Lord, just please don't let anyone else try to make me feel bad about my choices. Please help me remember I'm a working mom and proud of it. Thanks.

PRAYER

for My Maternity Leave II

❤

Dear God, Is nine weeks of maternity leave ever enough? Don't get me wrong—I love my job and I can't wait to dig in again. But I'm just not ready to leave my babe, not yet. I pumped and banked my milk, but my little guy still won't take a bottle. Can I really just hope he'll cave in and take the bottle when Mommy's breasts aren't around? My nanny's ready and waiting to take him in. But am I ready to turn over my precious bundle to another woman for ten hours a day, even one as highly recommended and thoroughly vetted as she is? And I can't possibly show anyone else how to do our walk-jiggle-hum routine that he needs before his nap, but how will he sleep without it? Lord, I said all along I didn't want to feel guilty about going back to work, but now I'm feeling heartbroken, and that's worse. Please send me emotional strength and killer organizational skills to live these last days of maternity leave to their fullest. Please help me remember I'm a working mom and proud of it. Thanks.

PRAYER

for My Mom, Too Close to Home

♥

Dear God, My mother is driving me crazy. Yes, I just had a child—her first grandbaby—and yes, we could use a little help. Just not this kind of help! She's crammed our tiny apartment with *stuff*—frilly outfits we wouldn't dream of putting on our daughter, toys she won't be able to play with till years from now, dozens of onesies, hundreds of baby wipes, and cases of infant formula, even though she knows I'm nursing exclusively. She covers her mouth with both hands in fear every time my husband picks the baby up, which is starting to piss him off (and why shouldn't it?), and she's cooked us straight out of our kitchen. A little food on hand would be great, but three lasagnas, a beef stew, and a double-wide shepherd's pie? Just no. Last week she roasted an entire turkey dinner—in June!—when all I wanted was hummus and pita chips and a stolen sip of chardonnay. Lord, please help her to realize her granddaughter's going to be in her life for the rest of her life, so she doesn't need to do it all now. Truly, Lord, I know we're blessed to have my mom so close, and there's no feeling on earth like seeing her with my baby and the both of them so happy. Now if we could just do something about the two gallons of chicken soup on the stove, we'd be much obliged. Thanks, Lord.

PRAYER

for My Mom, So Far Away

❤

Dear God, My mother is breaking my heart. Why won't she come visit? I just had a child! Her first grandbaby! I could use a little help. But she's in Arizona with her cranky second husband, and I'm here, thousands of miles away and missing her. Oh, we had a lovely "virtual shower" beforehand, but it's not the same as having your mom drop by with all the little day-to-day things you need—onesies and baby wipes and a can or two of formula to have on hand, just in case the nursing isn't working out. She loaded us up with gift cards to all our favorite takeout places, but it's not the same as eating lasagna or beef stew or shepherd's pie made by your very own mom. Last night I had the oddest craving for my mother's roast turkey dinner—and it's June! I miss her so much, Lord. Now that I'm a mom, I want my own mother more than ever. Please help me to remember that my daughter will be her granddaughter for the rest of her life, and that, much as I want her here, she doesn't need to do it all now.

Truly, Lord, I know I'm blessed to be here and healthy and safe with my husband and my baby, knowing my mother is thinking of us from far away. Now if You could just do something about this craving I'm having for her homemade chicken soup, I'd be much obliged. Thanks, Lord.

PRAYER

for My Boss

♥

Dear God, Here we go. I'm up for my biannual performance review today, six months to the *minute* after I returned from maternity leave. God, please bless my boss with the wisdom of Solomon and the patience of Job as she reviews my goals and objectives. I admire her and I like working for her, but she's a hard driver. And truth be told, these have not been the hardest-driving months of my career, what with a sleepless baby, an exhausted husband, and a neglected dog at home. Please help her remember what these early days are like, even though when her kids were young, she had a fabulous nanny; a fabulous au pair for when the fabulous nanny was off; and a fabulous husband to negotiate between the nanny and the au pair. I have expensive, inflexible day care, a well-meaning mother-in-law, and an under-organized, overworked husband. Please help her remember all the great work I've done over the years, and forget the three days in a row when I came in late (okay, very late) and left early (okay, very early) when my baby had that rotavirus infection. Please stop her from making any subliminal judgment calls about my fat clothes, old shoes, and lack of manicure (her nails are always perfect—when does she find the time?). Please remind her that babies don't stay young forever, and even disorganized mothers like me eventually get the hang of this work-kid-sleep thing. Fill her with empathy, could you, Lord? Because I like this job. And I really need it—diapers are *expensive*. Thanks.

PRAYER
for My Grandmother

❤

Dear God, Please bless and protect my beloved Gram, especially now. Look at how happy she is, back in her own home after all those weeks in the hospital, playing with my baby. Her seventh great-grandchild! Please give me the same patience and grace you seem to have given her—to accept that she's at the end of the journey, that it's only hospice from here on in. Thank you for giving her, and me, and my daughter this time together, with Gram at the very end of things and my little girl just starting out. Not to sound like a Disney soundtrack or anything, but it really is a circle of life, isn't it? Thank you for giving me this family—my grandmother, my mom, and now my baby girl, staggering around on her chubby legs, her little toes gripping the 1960s linoleum that Gram never felt she needed to upgrade. Thank you for letting me have my grandmother in my life as long as I have. And thank you for giving her the time to see her last grandbaby learn how to walk. Please give my little girl some of her great-gram's grace and good humor, and please help me be strong when you-know-what happens. I'm going to need it. Thanks, Lord.

PRAYER

at the Two-Month Checkup

❤

Dear God, Am I doing the right thing? My brain is a bit fried right now, what with the zero sleep for fifty-six days in a row (not that I'm counting or anything). Now I'm perched in here with my little bean in her bucket—yes, completely covered up so she doesn't catch anything from this nasty waiting room—and I just can't stop worrying. Is this the right thing, shooting all these shots into a tiny little thirteen-pound eleven-ounce body? HepB and RV and Diap and Hb and PCV and IPV—really? All now? I understand the importance of vaccines to the community and the individual, but look at my little peach-pit's legs. They're still so skinny. Do we really want to put a needle in there, a whole series of needles? Into her tiny arms, so fragile and so perfect? Can't I just keep her really, really close to me for, like, ever? Can't *I* be her vaccine? If not, God, would you mind? Can *you* be her vaccine—keep her safe from the diseases, but also safe from all this medicine that may or may not have been properly double-blind tested? I'm officially surrendering to your will here, Lord. Please tell me this is the right thing to do. Thanks.

PRAYER

for My Baby's First Step

❤

Dear God, It happened! He walked! I swear, he just took his first real, unsupported step. He looked me right in the eye, let go of the coffee table, and took two steps before he fell. I don't mean to gush, but this little guy is on his game, I've said it all along. You can just tell by that spark in his eye that he's ready to go. I could already tell from his nonstop pulling-up and lap-standing that he was going to walk early, and here he is, just eleven months old and taking his first steps. Thank you, Lord, for giving us such a sturdy and strong son. Thank you for keeping him healthy and thriving. I know how lucky we are. Please let this be the beginning for him of an active, engaged life. I can tell already he's a real go-getter. Please let him always use his agility in the best possible ways. Do you think he might be a pilot or a fire-fighter or a wildlife ranger or a basketball player? Maybe another basketball-playing president of the United States? Am I dreaming too big? I would ask that he never gets hurt, but I know that's just plain unrealistic. So instead, Lord, can you make it so that, however many risks he takes, he'll always remember the tentativeness of these first precious steps and how his mom was right by his side to keep him safe? Thanks, God.

PRAYER

upon Bringing Our Second Baby Home

●

Dear God, Hoo boy. This is the tough part—well, the emergency C-section was tough, too, but this is tough in a different way. Here we are, walking through the door with beautiful Baby No. 2, and the look on her big brother's face is enough to make me call for another round of postpartum drugs. Oh, we've talked this all through, but no amount of words can change what's just happened. He used to be the center of the universe, now he's just a star—a very very bright star, but now only one of a pair. As the joke goes, you'd be upset too, if your husband told you he loved you so much he wanted to have another wife "just like you!" Lord, I know we'll all be just fine in the long run. But right now, looking at my firstborn's beloved face, I do miss the awesome threesome that we were for those twenty-seven sweet and blissful months. Please let my two children love one another as they're growing up, and also as adults. Please let my son relax and forget about this "stupid baby," as he just called her. Help him go back to his blocks and his books and his TV shows and the whole wonderful world he's created for himself. And please, Lord, could you help my Big Boy to hug his infant sister a little less enthusiastically than he's doing right this very instant? Because if I didn't know better, God, I'd swear he was trying to squeeze the life right out of her. But he's not, right? Right?

PRAYER

for the Birthday Cake 1

○

Dear God, Help. The pirate cake is falling apart. The one I spent three-plus hours on this morning. The one my three-year-old begged and begged me to make for his big day. Even though I told him in advance the gunwales made of milk-chocolate wafer rolls were not going to stick to the deck with just a dab of icing. We followed every direction, Lord: We baked and cooled and cut and layered and trimmed and iced and bolstered various structural bits with drinking straws and wooden dowels. But now, as we are loading it oh-so-carefully into the car, it's falling apart before our eyes. The center cannot hold. Mere anarchy is loosed upon my child's birthday. The vanilla cookie planking is separating from the mast. The root-beer-barrel candies are rolling off the cake-stand entirely. The birthday boy is in tears, and the birthday boy's mother feels the need for a large tumbler of scotch, no ice, even though it is not quite noon. Lord, am I a bad parent for suggesting we destroy this

TRACY MAYOR

bugger right here and now, have the two of us attack it with a couple of forks? I try to roll with the punches, God, and I do my best to raise a kid who's able to handle disappointment without falling apart. But a foundering pirate cake is just too much. We're going overboard, God, stand clear as we prepare to sink this sucker.

PRAYER

for the Birthday Cake 11

○

Dear God, Okay, we've recovered, and we're moving on to Plan
B. Plan A—the most fabulous pirate cake ever baked—fell apart
in the car and in retribution we have at least partially devoured
it. Now we're jacked up on sugar and able to think quickly,
which is key if we're going to have cake to serve to twenty-two
three-year-olds an hour from now at what I am quickly coming
to think of as the Birthday Party from Hell. So, please God, let
our local Carvel have an abundant supply of Fudgie the Whale
cakes. Yes, it's somewhat humiliating, perhaps even acutely humiliating, to serve prepackaged foodstuffs advertised on television to this particular crowd of hot mamas and their high-end
offspring, who are used to the best of everything. But this is as
good as it's going to get, God, so I'm asking you to make it good
enough. Please let those little dudes and dudesses squeal with
delight when we bring forth the whales, so my little guy doesn't

feel inadequate on his big day. We're pulling into the parking lot now, Lord. Please let there be whales to be had. Because that's my Plan B, and I don't have a Plan C. Thanks, God.

PRAYER
for My Baby's First Word

💙

Dear God, It happened! She talked! I swear, she said her first word, and I swear, it was "Mama." She looked me right in the eye, held out her cookie to me, and said, "Mama." I don't mean to gush, but this girl is on her game, I've said it all along. You can just tell by that spark in her eye that she's ready to go. I could already tell from the nonstop babbling that she's going to be a real chatterbox, just like her mom. Thank you, Lord, for giving us such an alert and engaged child. Thank you for keeping her healthy and thriving. I know how lucky we are. Please let this be the beginning for her of a long love affair with words. I can tell already that she's a real communicator. Please let her always use her verbal gifts in the best possible ways. Do you think she might be a doctor, or a diplomat, or a university president? Maybe *the* president? Am I dreaming too big? I would ask that we never have any bad words between us, but I know

TRACY MAYOR

that's just plain unrealistic. So instead, Lord, can you make it so that, however bad things get between teenaged her and menopausal me, we'll both always remember this awesome moment and how "Mama" was her very first word? Thanks, God.

PRAYER

for Moms Who Work from Home

Dear God, This seemed like such a great idea in theory. Sitting in my boss's office, peering at her over the enormous mound of my first child still in utero, I felt truly inspired in proposing my brilliant work-from-home scheme. And I was good, Lord, because she bought it. But now it's my first week back in the saddle, "working" from my newly renovated closet-turned-office, and there's just one problem: There's an infant in the house! What was I thinking? I was imagining . . . sleep. Silence. Peaceful hours of baby cooing quietly at the ceiling, lulled by the sound of my productive-working-mother typing. What I have is a kid who doesn't like to be put down for a second, who nurses every hour, who has killed off every functioning brain cell left in my cerebellum. Right this moment she's arm's-length away in her swing, which is cranked on ultra-high, and I'm sitting in front of the computer with a pile of squeaky toys in my lap. When she fusses, I toss another her way (don't worry, they only *sometimes* bonk her right in her soft baby skull). When that pile runs out, the workday is over with, which should clock me in at about . . . twenty-five minutes for the day. These are the early days, Lord—please give my boss patience while my baby and I settle into a routine. Please give me back my once-mighty organizational skills so I can get all this work and mothering stuff done. And please make my babe be one of the ones who really, really loves being in her swing. Thanks, Lord.

PRAYER
for My Old Boyfriend

Dear God, Well, it happened. I knew that sooner or later I'd run into my ex, and today I did. I had my adorable baby and my hot husband with me, so thank you for that. I try to be virtuous, Lord, but I have not yet fully risen above a primal need for revenge. On the downside, I happened to be wearing my son in a backpack, which is a bummer because those things manage to make your boobs, your waist, and your butt all look wrong at the same moment. I hope my ex wasn't looking at any of those body parts, though you know what a fixation he always had. I hope he was looking at my face, so he could see how content and confident I am now. I hope my aura was shining through, Lord, because, at the end of the day—even at the end of some of these very long baby days—I am a lucky woman and a grateful mama. Thank you for this happiness, God, and thank you for not letting me marry that jerk. Amen.

TRACY MAYOR

PRAYER
for Barbie

Dear God, Well, here she is in all her ponytailed plastic glory, Barbie herself. She of the freakish 36-18-33 body measurements and Malibu tan and the 10,000 pink accessories sold separately, including tiny stiletto heels that get sucked up by the vacuum in no time flat. The doll I swore would never darken our doorstep is inside, unpackaged, and currently having her Hot Tub Party House Vehicle play set assembled, all thanks to my in-laws. So much for that moratorium. God, please don't make this be the biggest mistake of my young parenting life. My girl is only three, but I've worked hard already to make sure she's the most self-assured, pro-girl kid on the playground. Please don't let this stupid doll undo any of that. My cutie prances around with her hair in a hideous rat's nest, her little baby belly hanging over the top of her too-small tutu, her chubby thighs rubbing together as she shimmies. If Barbie screws up any of that beautiful body image, I will cut her. I'm not naïve, Lord. I know this is only the beginning of a long struggle with a toxic popular culture that leaks in and around the little bubble of safe, happy self-esteem we've created for our girl. Please give me the patience to endure these fads without over-reacting, and please give me the wisdom to know when I should react. Also the foresight not to vacuum up those expensive accessories. Thanks, God.

PRAYER

for My Little Flower Girl

Dear God, Why did I agree to this? Because I was helpless in the face of a relentless Bridezilla? Because I was honestly touched by her request? Because—and I'll admit it—a little part of me wanted my adorable, captivating three-year-old to be the center of attention, if only for the short walk down the aisle? How about all of the above? The only problem, Lord, is that *none* of the above is happening. Oh, my daughter is exquisitely turned out, as she should be for the $190 we forked over for her dress and the $44 we paid for her patent-leather shoes. But when my girl got a look at the size of the crowd, she freaked—and who can blame her, with 180 people looking over their shoulders and saying "Aww" simultaneously? Lord, I promise I'll never again put my daughter on show if you can somehow fix it so I don't have to walk down that aisle with her right now. I'm wearing a borrowed dress in a bad color with an unflattering drape! The focus was always supposed to be on my girl, not me. But she's not budging, Lord. The bride is already in the back of the church, getting poufed. Her dad is looking at his watch. The wedding planner with the lacquered hair is making a frantic sweeping motion in our direction. No last-minute miracles from you? Okay, God, it looks like we're going to walk the walk together. Here we go, wish us luck.

TRACY MAYOR

PRAYER

for December 26

Dear God, Do these religious holidays exhaust you as much as they exhaust us? Are you, like, a mess after Ramadan or in need of a day in bed after Rosh Hashanah? Because it's December 26, I am utterly beat, and our house looks like a bomb went off in every room. I'm not complaining, Lord, because most of this Christmas season has been so magical with little ones in the house. It's enormously fun to play Santa and buy their presents in secret. Singing the old, beautiful Christmas carols with them, and watching their eyes widen when we talk about how a baby came to save the whole world, it's rapturous. And the lights—just seeing my baby mesmerized by the lights that are everywhere, that's reason enough for the season. And yet, Lord, there is the endless cooking and cleaning and shopping and wrapping and mailing and making sure everyone we've ever met receives our family photo card, which took me four hours at the computer to get perfect. And then there are the family dynamics to navigate, already tricky but made far trickier now that precious grandbabies are in the mix. Now it's over, God, for this year at least, and I'm feeling deeply grateful and deeply spent. Thank you for the Christmas season, and thank you that it only comes once a year. Amen.

PRAYER

for Single Moms

Dear God, The next time my well-meaning friend says, "My husband travels so much I might as well be a single parent," could you do me a quick favor and smite her halfway to hell and back? I love her, but she is so *not* a single parent. She shouldn't be allowed to even utter the phrase. I *am* a single parent—as you know, Lord, from my very frequent entreaties—and I'm only too familiar with the single-mommy drill: never feeling like everything is done, never feeling like you can catch a break, never feeling free to let your guard down, always feeling judged to a higher standard, always worrying about the bank account, the shopping, the laundry, the preschool tuition, the job, the college savings fund, and most of all, the physical and emotional well-being of my daughter. I love my little girl, and we're doing great together, but that doesn't mean I don't fantasize about hearing another adult ask in a sweet and sexy voice at the end of a long day, "What should I make us for dinner?" I know you've put a lot of love in this world, and I know a piece of it has my name on it, somewhere and somehow. I'm not afraid to wait for it patiently. In the meantime, Lord, please grant me respite from all the little looks and crappy assumptions that get dumped on single moms and their kids. And especially save me from my married friends and their clueless whining. Thanks, God.

TRACY MAYOR

PRAYER

for My Maternity Clothes

◆

Dear God, Please bless these maternity clothes as I wash, dry, fold, and pack them up for the Goodwill van, which will take them the heck out of my life. I loved them because I loved being pregnant—both times—and they were my badge of honor. And I hated them because I was thoroughly sick of them by the time I delivered, both times. And that's not even considering those hellish couple of weeks after delivery when I was still too big to fit into my regular clothes. Good-bye, sleeveless baby-doll blouse that I wore when I was boiling hot, which was always. Good-bye, faux-wrap white poplin shirt, which was the closest thing I could find to a business look. Good-bye underbelly five-pocket boot-cut dark wash jeans from a Famous Designer. You cost an insane amount of money for maternity wear, yet your hipness saved my sanity, so you were well worth every penny. Good-bye elbow-sleeve empire-waist dress that I wore almost every Monday, Wednesday, and Friday to work because I was too frugal to spring for a bigger maternity wardrobe. You, I won't miss at all. And finally, good-bye smocked-waist maternity tankini. In a weird way, you were the most comfortable bathing suit I've ever owned, only because I was finally free to let it all hang out at the beach. Now some other moms-to-be are going to let it hang out. Lord, let them be as happy as I was. Let their pregnancies go as smoothly, and when it's all over, let them fit back into their regular jeans as soon as possible. Thanks, God.

PRAYER

before My Mother-in-Law's Visit

Dear God, As you may know, my beloved mother-in-law is winging her way north from Florida at this very moment for her yearly one-week visit. Please grant me seven days of infinite patience, endless good humor, and a really clean kitchen. I truly am grateful that you've granted me such a sane mother-in-law; from what my girlfriends tell me, this is not always the case, so thanks for that. Still, it's nerve-wracking to have an older woman—let's even use the phrase "neat freak"—staying under your roof when you've got a baby to nurse and a toddler to entertain. Please let her see how clean the bathrooms are— all at the same time!—and please let her not notice the mold on the ceiling. Please let her see that all the throw pillows she's sent us over the years, even the very ugly ones, are nicely displayed on the couch. And please let her not notice they're there to cover up the stains from the cat pee. Please let her be so distracted by all her tchotchkes in our kitchen (taken from under the sink just for her visit) that she doesn't notice the finger-prints on the fridge door, the greasy hood over the range that I didn't have time to clean, or the baseboard paint chipped by repeated run-ins from a Tonka truck. Let me always remember that she raised the great guy I have started a family with. In particular, please let me remember that when I come down early some morning to find her already up and cleaning the bottom of our toaster oven. Thanks, God.

PRAYER

for the Halloween Costume 1

♥

Dear God, Does this look like a ladybug to you? Because to me it looks like a cross between a toadstool and SpongeBob SquarePants. And judging from the tears streaming down my toddler's face, it's not working for her either. I'm a creative mom, Lord, you know that. We've got the cupboards stuffed full of markers, crayons, glue, stickers, felt scraps, buttons, ribbon, popsicle sticks, and googly eyes. But I swear, Lord, this Halloween costume business is simply beyond my parenting capabilities. Who are these mothers with their perfect homemade costumes? When do they start these projects—New Year's Day? Every year October 31 sneaks up on me, and every year my darling child winds up having to tell everyone what she's *supposed* to be—a sure sign I flunked costume-making once again. So, God, this year if you don't mind, could you please make this getup somehow magically look like a ladybug so my girl will stop crying and the other moms will stop judging? I don't mean to be ungrateful, but who invented this holiday anyhow, some crazy pagans? Because it's tough on moms, I'm just saying.

PRAYER

for the Halloween Costume II

●

Dear Lord, Yes I am aware that it's October 30 at 6:30 P.M. and that this is not an ideal time to find prime selection at the uPartyMart Costume Center and Paper Goods Supply Warehouse. God, you cannot guess the depths of my regret that life has led me to this point. If I repent—if I promise to start on next year's costume on, say, New Year's Day—would it somehow be possible to do some Godly thing and restock these bare shelves with superhero costumes in the right size so my toddler will stop weeping face-down in the aisle, as he is currently doing? Just one or two would be fine—maybe a Batman with the fake rock-hard abs? Or a ninja with a sword that's realistic enough to impress the three-year-olds, but not enough to get us kicked out of the preschool party ("No weapons, no scary masks, no fake blood, please")? Also, any way you could make his costume of choice somehow look homemade? Or at least high-end, like the fifty-dollar outfits from the schmancy kids' clothing catalog? Because I just know the other moms will judge my kid by his crummy and cheap last-minute costume, and it's not the poor kid's fault his mom is a Halloween failure. I'm trying not to complain here, Lord, but who invented this holiday anyhow, some crazy pagans? Because it's tough on moms, I'm just saying.

PRAYER

for Stay-at-Home Moms

●

Dear God, Most days I'm so happy to be staying home with my kids, and so grateful I can do it. But some days—the dark, rainy, long ones with multiple meltdowns and runny diapers and piles of laundry and too many games of Candyland—I do long for a clean, well-lit office, a coffeemaker that's always on, adults to talk to, and a job with a clear set of goals and objectives. What are my goals and objectives now? Get through the day, and then get through the next. Run the entire household—and because we're down to one salary, run it on a dime. Be there for my kids—be the one who's there when they wake up, the one who helps them navigate the social frustrations of the park and the library, the one who plays here-comes-the-airplane in the high chair and sings them to sleep for their naps. I love all of this, and I chose it, even though I know it means no budget for new clothes for the next decade or so. All I need, God, is a short, witty reply when people ask me what I "do," one that doesn't make me sound defensive, stupid, or like some kind of militant post-feminist mommybot. Help me to truly believe that work is always out there if I want it, but for now, my work is here. Thanks, God.

PRAYER

for Adoptive Moms

●

Dear God, Thank you for my family. Thank you for blessing my husband and me with these two daughters, who fill us with more joy than we ever could have imagined. As you must recall, thanks to my incessant prayers over the past four years, it's been a long, long journey—emotionally and physically—to parenthood for us. But worth every moment, even the very discouraging ones. And now we are so very happy, and we feel so very settled as a family. So thank you for all that, Lord. Now if I could make just one last request, I'll stop bugging you: Can you somehow stop people from asking, "Are they *yours*?" in a tone that implies we picked them up in a two-for-one deal from Costco? While you're at it, go ahead and ban "Who is her *real* mother?" (*I* am her real mother! The term you're looking for is "birth mother.") Also, feel free to strike mute the people who ask how much our girls "cost," why their birth mothers "gave them up," or which of us was infertile. (Trust me, people, if I

wanted to talk plumbing with you, I'd be carrying a plunger.)
Lord, I know people are well intentioned—well, most of the
time. Help me to remember that they're naturally curious
about our slightly unconventional family. If I promise to try
and respond with grace and humor, can you stop them from
being quite so tactless and dumb? Thanks for that bargain,
God, and thanks again for my adopted kids.

PRAYER

for the Dad without the Diaper Bag

●

Dear God, The man is trying, we have to give him credit. He's home from work today, taking both of our kids to their Baby n' Me swim classes. All on his own, he packed the diaper bag with three swimsuits, two swim diapers, three regular diapers for later, skin cream, shampoo, baby Crocs, hooded duckie towels, an adult towel, and age- and diet-appropriate snacks and drinks for everyone. There's just one problem: The diaper bag is *here,* in our front hallway, and he's halfway down the street already. I'd call him, but his phone's in the diaper bag as well. As you know, God, my husband is someone who's previously traveled with very little baggage. Now, thanks to his two beloved kids, he's burdened with more crap than he's ever before needed to keep track of. Please give my husband the patience of Job when he realizes his mistake. Help him to realize that he can salvage the morning with a detour to the doughnut shop, which is more fun than swim class anyhow. And, Lord, please let him at least have his wallet on him. Thank you.

PRAYER

for Special Needs Moms

Dear God, I am not "a saint." I am not "amazing," "wonderful," or "special." I am, as you know from my near-constant prayers, the mother of a disabled child. If one more person tells me that this somehow makes me a better mother than she is—magically more able to handle it than she'd be—I'm going to smack her upside the head. My husband and I deal with our little guy's physical and mental disabilities the way any other parent would: We do what we have to, even when it's incredibly frustrating and exhausting and heartbreaking. I've made my peace with it, and with you, Lord. Now help me make peace with the world—with the people who turn away from us in public, or the people who make those big cow eyes of sympathy, or the real kicker, with the people who say, in that hushed voice, that You somehow chose me because I was stronger than all those mommies with typical babies. Puleeze! I never would have chosen this, but it's the road we're on, for better or worse. Thank you for standing by me when I'm raging with anger, or broken down with sorrow, or, more often than you'd think, doubled over with laughter at the absurdity of my life. Thank you for giving my husband and me moments of real joy, lots of them, with our boy. And thank you for not holding it against me when I tell those other mothers, even just in my mind, to "stuff it." Thanks, God, and amen.

TRACY MAYOR

PRAYER

for Right Here, Right Now

Dear God, What did my great aunt tell me right after my first baby was born? "The days might drag, but the years go by quick." Boy was she ever right! Some days absolutely do drag on—an exhausted jumble of runny diapers and sticky high chairs, sick sitters and snide bosses and stubborn strollers, meltdowns and showdowns and time-outs, naps and snacks, baths, and bed. Other days, the pure light of heaven seems to shine down on everything we do—dancing and giggling and building forts with the sofa cushions, finger-painting and dressing up and singing at the top of our lungs, eating peanut butter off the spoon and ice cream straight from the carton. It only takes a few leaf piles and snowstorms and rain puddles and sunny summer Sundays for a whole year to somehow fly by. And without my quite realizing it, my baby is a toddler and my toddler is a preschooler. Thank you for this life, Lord, however fast it might be rushing past. Thank you for making me a mother. Thank you for my children, whichever way we found each other. Thank you for my family, however typical or unconventional we may be. Bless us and keep us safe, and help me always to remember how precious our days are together. Even the crappy ones. Amen.

ACKNOWLEDGMENTS

Thanks to Leslie Wells at Hyperion; Dan Lazar at Writer's House; Stephanie Wilkinson and Jennifer Niesslein, who started this prayer chain in the pages of *Brain,Child* magazine; Kate Trump O'Connor for her insight on special needs moms; Nic, Claire, Whitney, Donna, Jen, Walter, Jen, and my other writer/parent/friends who provided ideas and inspiration; and my parents and brothers, who taught me first how funny families could be.

Mother and blogger TRACY MAYOR is an editor at Brain, Child magazine and has written for a variety of websites and publications, including Salon.com, the Boston Globe Magazine and Child. She lives north of Boston.